Blue Banner Biography

Akon

Mary Boone

Mitchell Lane
PUBLISHERS

P.O. Box 196
Hockessin, Delaware 19707
Visit us on the web: www.mitchelllane.com
Comments? email us: mitchelllane@mitchelllane.com

Printing   1   2   3   4   5   6   7   8   9

Blue Banner Biographies

Akon
Allen Iverson
Ashton Kutcher
Beyoncé
Carrie Underwood
Christina Aguilera
Clay Aiken
David Ortiz
Eve
Gwen Stefani
Ja Rule
Jessica Simpson
JoJo
Kate Hudson
Kenny Chesney
Mariah Carey
Mary-Kate and Ashley Olsen
Missy Elliott
Orlando Bloom
Peyton Manning
Rudy Giuliani
Shakira
Usher

Alan Jackson
Ashanti
Avril Lavigne
Bow Wow
Chris Brown
Christopher Paul Curtis
Condoleezza Rice
Derek Jeter
Fergie (Stacy Ferguson)
Ice Cube
Jay-Z
J. K. Rowling
Justin Berfield
Keith Urban
Lance Armstrong
Mario
Michael Jackson
Nancy Pelosi
P. Diddy
Queen Latifah
Sally Field
Shirley Temple
Zac Efron

Alicia Keys
Ashlee Simpson
Bernie Mac
Britney Spears
Chris Daughtry
Ciara
Daniel Radcliffe
Eminem
50 Cent
Jamie Foxx
Jennifer Lopez
Johnny Depp
Justin Timberlake
Kelly Clarkson
Lindsay Lohan
Mary J. Blige
Miguel Tejada
Nelly
Paris Hilton
Ron Howard
Selena
Tim McGraw

Library of Congress Cataloging-in-Publication Data
Boone, Mary.
    Akon / by Mary Boone.
        p. cm. — (Blue banner biographies)
    Includes bibliographical references (p.   ), discography (p.   ), and index.
    ISBN 978-1-58415-630-7 (library bound)
    1. Akon (Rapper)—Juvenile literature. 2. Rap musicians—United States—Biography—Juvenile literature. I. Title.
    ML3930.A39B66 2008
    782.421649092—dc22
    [B]

782.4216
BOO 4/08

                                                                                        2007019688

ABOUT THE AUTHOR: Mary Boone has written over a dozen books for young adults, including biographies about Hilary Duff, Lindsay Lohan, and Raven. She also has written for magazines including *People, Teen People, Mary-Kate and Ashley,* and *Entertainment Weekly.* Boone lives in Tacoma, Washington. When she's not writing she enjoys running, swimming, and being outdoors with her husband, Mitch, and their two children, Eve and Eli.

PHOTO CREDITS: Cover, p. 12—Nina Prommer/Globe Photos; pp. 4, 25—Ray Tamarra/Getty Images; p. 7—Ethan Miller/Getty Images; p. 10—Uri Schanker/Getty Images; p. 17—Kevin Winter/Getty Images; p. 18—Amy Sussman/Getty Images; p. 21—Frank Micelotta/Getty Images; p. 27—MTV/Getty Images.

                                                                                        PPC

Akon poses for an artist's portrait in October 2006. The singer, whose music defies traditional labels, has found success with hard-luck stories, beat-heavy raps, and dance floor favorites.

Bumpy Beginnings

*A*liaune Thiam (pronounced CHAHM) was a New Jersey high school student when his father got a job teaching at Clark Atlanta University in Georgia. His parents moved 900 miles away, leaving teenage Aliaune and his older brother with a house and a car to themselves.

"We had too much freedom," Aliaune told *The Washington Post.*

He went to classes and a friend tried to teach him to sing reggae but, with no parents around to watch over him, Aliaune fell in with the wrong crowd. He started selling test answers and quickly moved up to dealing marijuana out of his locker. A friend gave him a .22; soon he was renting the gun out for $100 a day. He stole cars and resold them to drug dealers.

Before long, Aliaune's illegal behavior caught up with him. He was expelled and spent time in juvenile detention before eventually transferring to and graduating from another school. He moved to Georgia for college but dropped out after just one year. He picked up music again and was thrilled to get a deal with Elektra/East West Records. When label executives dropped him almost as quickly as they signed him, he returned to his criminal ways.

Aliaune started stealing and selling luxury cars. He got other guys to steal cars, too. Soon he was the head of a major car-theft ring with hubs in Chicago, New Jersey, and Atlanta. "I was posing as an entertainer," Aliaune told *Vibe* magazine. "So, when (people) asked me 'Where'd you get this money?' I was like, 'I produce. I have studios, recording artists.' "

Not everyone bought his lie. In 1999, federal agents charged Aliaune with being the ringleader of a national car-theft operation. He spent three years in prison—and now counts that time behind bars as a blessing.

"I felt like God was really looking out for me," he told *The Washington Post.* "I'm trying to figure out why I'm even in here. I had no reason. I was never that type of guy. I was always the coolest dude you're ever going to meet, I was brought up by a great family, I had a great future, what . . . am I doing? I was trippin'. Every day, I'm crying, talking to God, saying: 'If you get me out this situation, I promise, I'm never getting back in it.' "

Aliaune Thiam stayed true to that promise. Within a

> **"Every day, I'm crying, talking to God, saying: 'If you get me out this situation, I promise, I'm never getting back in it.' "**

Akon, right, performs with Snoop Dog during the 2006 American Music Awards. The duo's song, "I Want to Love You," received two 2007 BET award nominations.

few years, the one-time car thief became known as Akon, a controversial R&B artist who fills concert halls and collaborates with big-name musicians like Eminem and Snoop Dog.

These days, Akon has millions of fans around the world, but it wasn't so long ago that he felt alone and friendless in his own neighborhood.

When Akon was born, his parents named him Aliaune Damala Bouga Time Puru Nacka Lu Lu Lu Badara Akon Thiam. He's chosen to go by one of his middle names.

His father, jazz percussionist Mor Thiam, and mother, dancer Kiné Thiam, left the Republic of Senegal in western Africa so that Mor could work with Katherine Dunham, an American dance legend.

SENEGAL

This map of Africa shows Senegal, highlighted in yellow. Akon was born in the United States but his parents were from Senegal, and he still travels there often.

Akon has kept many facets of his life secret. He won't talk about his age beyond saying he is the second-oldest of five children.

"I don't advertise my age because in this industry you are as young as you sound," he told Slamjamz.com. "Once you let people know your age in this business, that's when the countdown begins."

Akon was born after his parents moved to St. Louis, Missouri. When he was young, the Thiams divided their time between the United States and Senegal. Because of the frequent trips to Africa and the fact that his parents often spoke Senegal's national language, Wolof, at home, Akon didn't learn how to speak English as a small child. That language barrier kept his parents from enrolling him in kindergarten until he was seven—two years older than most other children.

Akon kept his age a secret, but his classmates couldn't help noticing that his skin was much darker than theirs; for this, he was teased and taunted nearly every day. As his English improved, he gained an even clearer understanding of his classmates' cruelty. He struck back with his fists and found himself at the center of many childhood fights.

When Akon was in fifth grade, his family moved to Florida so that his father could teach music at the University of Miami. By then, Akon's language skills were well developed, but he still liked to pretend he couldn't speak English.

"I took advantage of being African," he told *Vibe*. "I never revealed the fact that I spoke English fluently. While they're talking about me, I'm listening, with them thinking I don't know what they're talking about."

Akon also liked to pretend he was an African prince. Fellow students watched in awe when his father picked him and his brothers up from school in a shiny, black Mercedes-Benz.

"Everybody believed every stereotype [about Africa]," he told *Vibe*. "I was like, 'These guys can't be no more stupid than they look.' " His family moved from Florida to New Jersey right after Eddie Murphy's *Coming to America* hit theaters. In that movie, Murphy plays an African prince who moves to Queens, New York, and pretends to be just a regular American guy. "That [movie] helped me even more," says Akon. "Everybody thought I was a prince."

A real prince? No. But Akon was on his way to becoming musical royalty.

> *"I never revealed the fact that I spoke English fluently. While they're talking about me, I'm listening."*

Akon takes center stage during the 2005 Hotel MTV concert in Miami. The singer, who's rarely without his bling, made news in early 2007 when he announced plans to overtake Guinness Book of World Records *inductee Lil' Jon by creating the biggest diamond pendant ever.*

Here Comes Trouble

*A*kon started messing around with music in high school. At first he made demo tapes, performing hit songs by some of his favorite artists. Before long, he was writing his own music.

In 1993, a friend in New Jersey introduced Akon to Wyclef Jean, a Grammy Award–winning rapper/reggae artist and member of the hip-hop trio The Fugees. Akon started hanging out at Wyclef's studio, The Booga Basement. 'Clef was so impressed with the young musician's vocal talent that he invited Akon to sit in with The Fugees when they recorded their 1996 best-selling album *The Score*. It was a big break, but it still wasn't enough to get Akon to give up his criminal ways.

Prison sidetracked Akon's musical career, but it also gave him time to think.

"That's what created everything you're hearing today — from my attitude to my music," he told *Entertainment*

When Akon was released from prison, he was ready to change his life. He teamed up with pal DeVyne Stephens to market, promote, and distribute his music. Stephens entered the music business as a rap artist; before getting involved in artist development, he worked as a choreographer for artists including TLC, Usher, Toni Braxton, and Pink.

Weekly magazine. "All this happened when I got locked up—and woke up."

When he got out of prison in 2002, he had a new focus—and a felony record, which kept him from finding a traditional job in an office or factory. Desperate to turn things around, he got in touch with his old friend, choreographer and music developer DeVyne Stephens. The two got to work on what would eventually become Akon's first album. Writing and producing the music ended up being the simplest part of the process—selling it to a record executive was the hard part. The music wasn't pure hip-hop or R&B or rap. The fact that it couldn't easily be categorized scared off many labels.

But Steve Rifkind at SRC (Street Records Corporation) knew a good thing as soon as he heard it. "I lost my mind, jumped on a plane, flew to Atlanta, and had the deal done within 24 hours," Rifkind told *Vibe.* And, rather than hide Akon's unlawful past, the new label encouraged him to lyrically embrace it.

Rifkind's gamble paid off. Akon's debut CD, *Trouble,* went platinum (1 million copies sold) shortly after it was released in June 2004. Fans went crazy for the newcomer's songs about life in the hood, prison, and drug running. Critics couldn't stop writing about Akon's folk-like, nasally tenor voice.

Fans went crazy for the newcomer's songs about life in the hood, prison, and drug running.

"It's so unique," Lisa Ivery, program director for XM Satellite Radio's hip-hop and R&B channel, The City, told *The Washington Post.* "If you went to West Africa, to Senegal, you might find some people who sound similar to him. But not here."

His pal Wyclef Jean says Akon's voice represents the world. "Whether he's singing a girl record, a [hard-driving] record, or a 'the world must change' record,' his voice is the world," he told *Vibe.* "It defines no area. You can hear it in London, Brooklyn, Atlanta, Africa."

The fusion of Akon's distinctive voice and today's urban music proved a winning combination. His first single, "Locked Up," stayed in the Top 10 for more than eight

Akon's breakout song, 2004's "Locked Up," found the singer warbling about his stint behind bars. Critics praised his sweet falsetto and the tune spent two months in Billboard's Top 10.

weeks. It was one of the tunes he wrote while behind bars and proved a powerful testament to life in prison:

> *Visitation no longer comes by*
> *Seems like they forgot about me*
> *Commissary is getting empty*
> *My cell mates getting food without me*
> *Can't wait to get out and move forward with my life*
> *Got a family that loves me and wants me to do right*
> *But instead I'm here locked up*

The single "Sole Survivor" by Young Jeezy featuring Akon became a dance-club favorite, and "Lonely," a remake of a 1964 Bobby Vinton hit, soared to No. 1 in both the United Kingdom and Australia. "Ghetto," a tribute to his manager Robert Montanez who was shot dead in a dispute in New Jersey, also won rave reviews. The remix of the song became even more popular and propelled sales after verses from rappers 2Pac and The Notorious B.I.G. were added to it.

Trouble was a bona fide widespread hit, and suddenly Akon was selling as many albums as big-name stars like Justin Timberlake and Ciara. The album's long life and multiple hit singles resulted in total sales of more than 3 million copies.

Not one to rest on his laurels, Akon spent much of 2006 in the studio, working on a follow-up to his successful debut album.

When Akon's album *Konvicted* was released in November 2006, it debuted at No. 2 on Billboard's Top Albums chart and outsold most of its holiday season competition. The album was certified platinum (1 million copies sold) within five weeks of its release.

The album yielded a number of hits, including "Smack That," a raunchy duet with Eminem that went to No. 1 and broke the Billboard Hot 100 record in October 2006 for the largest one-week climb in the chart's 48-year history. The "Smack That" ringtone went platinum faster than almost any other since the Recording Industry Association of American started certifying them in 2004. It also earned Akon his first Grammy nomination for best rap/sung collaboration.

More important than record sales and award nominations, *Konvicted* help cement Akon along with Nelly, Eminem, and 50 Cent as the most successful urban artists of the decade.

> *"Smack That" earned Akon his first Grammy nomination for best rap/sung collaboration.*

Personal Convictions

Many fans wrongly assume Akon's sophomore album refers to his time in prison; it doesn't. Rather, he says, it's a statement about his personal convictions, beliefs, and opinions.

"Pretty much I always felt like I was being convicted in some way," Akon told *Vibe.* "It was the hip-hop world that accepted me so I kept getting labeled as a rap artist. Then I got labeled a reggae artist. I have a lot of political ties with Africa, so some people thought I was a politician. People naturally assumed me to be a certain thing. . . . That's why I spell it with a 'K.' It's my personal convictions."

Akon's willingness to speak his mind has, on occasion, gotten him into trouble. In October 2006, Akon made headlines when he told radio talk show host Angie Martinez that he had three wives. "I'm a polygamist," he told the New York Hot 97 disc jockey. "I will have as many wives as I can afford to have. It can work. My dad has four wives."

Akon is no stranger to controversy. The musician made headlines in 2006 when he announced he practiced polygamy; he later recanted the story.

Akon later downplayed the announcement, explaining that having more than one wife is commonplace in Africa. When interviewers wouldn't let the topic drop, Akon tried denying his comments and eventually started ignoring questions about his relationships.

Less than a month after his radio confession, Akon told AllHipHop.com that his record label, Universal, forced him to stop talking about what he'd told Martinez.

"In the beginning it was cool because I said, 'Okay, I got enough fans out there, I got a lot of supporters, I can get open with them,' " he said. "But then after me and Angie had that conversation, situations started getting heated. It started affecting other people that had nothing to do with us. Because of that, [the label] said they don't want me to promote that aspect, and I can't talk about that too much because it's destroying other people's families and other things. I said, 'OK, no problem.'

Akon signs a T-shirt for the 2006 Giorgio Armani Go Red for World AIDS auction. He uses his star-power to raise money and attention for worthwhile causes.

"Unfortunately, this is the world we live in, people do judge you by your beliefs and how you think," Akon continued. "It's a free country, but it's really not free."

So, what does Akon believe in? Well, for starters, hard work.

He produced all but one of the tracks on *Konvicted* and has toured extensively in support of it. The artist gets by on minimal amounts of sleep, squeezing in naps when he flies from venue to venue.

"Regular Americans take things for granted," he told *Vibe*. "It's not to a point where I would ever get comfortable."

He also believes in doing something positive for Africa. Through the United for Africa foundation, the music star is helping build schools, hospitals, and recreation centers. Akon visits Senegal frequently, and in 2005 he was named that country's official Youth Ambassador. He also decided that his 2007 world tour would begin in Africa—not in America or Europe, as is generally the rule with big-name musicians. He also demanded that his record label let him film the video for the song "Mama Africa" in Ghana instead of on some Hollywood soundstage. Prior to filming, Akon's videographers hosted a two-week seminar to help that country's music video makers improve their skills.

> *"People do judge you by your beliefs and how you think. It's a free country, but it's really not free."*

Collaboration

*I*t didn't take long for smooth-sounding Akon to become an in-demand producer and featured vocalist, working with rappers including Young Jeezy, Rick Ross, Styles P., and Beenie Man. He also has worked with India Arie, Elton John, Ladysmith Black Mambazo, and R. Kelly. Sony-BMG North America chairman Clive Davis contacted Akon directly to see if he'd write some new songs for Whitney Houston's next album.

"I don't have no boundaries when it comes to the music thing," he told the *Calgary Sun*. "And I think that's a mistake a lot of artists make—they contain themselves in this box where they can't do anything outside of the genre they're known for and it limits you, period, from growing."

Akon started doing feature appearances when he was still struggling to get his songs played. Now, when he produces a track for another artist, his voice is automatically part of the deal.

Akon and Gwen Stefani perform "Sweet Escape" during TV's American Idol. *In 2007, the two mega-artists took their tour to arenas around the world. Akon has become famous for his collaborations as well as for his solo work.*

"The fun part about producing other artists is the fact that it isn't me," Akon told Canadian celebrity news web site Dose.ca. "I could make a record for myself in my sleep because I know what I want. But for other artists, it's almost like you have to mimic a particular sound to fit them. So, it's more of a creative process."

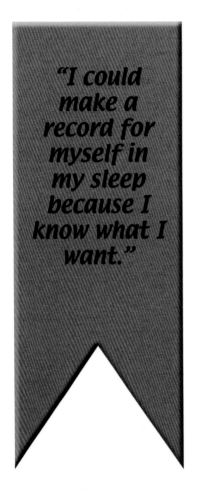

"I could make a record for myself in my sleep because I know what I want."

Akon recently teamed up with Gwen Stefani to produce "Sweet Escape." The breezy single climbed to No. 1 on the United World Chart. Their collaboration is the most challenging Akon has been part of—so far.

"I pretty much knew what she wanted to do, but . . . I wanted to bring her back toward the sound of [her former band] No Doubt," he told Dose.ca. "It was also about creating a track that I could hear myself on. I could hear myself doing a collaboration with No Doubt, so I wanted to give her that kind of a record to bring her back and to bring her older fans back."

In the end, the partnership succeeded. In addition to creating a hit record, Akon opened for Stefani's 2007 Sweet Escape Tour.

Akon's frequent collaborations have helped him build a network of friends throughout the music community. Those relationships paid off when he wanted to connect with Eminem on "Smack That."

"He was a hard guy to reach because he has so many people in front of him, that getting to him directly was almost impossible," Akon told *USA Today.* "But I had done a record for [Eminem's friend] Obie Trice, and that kind of opened the bridge for us to get together in the studio. It turns out we were fans of each other's work and I wound up doing some joints for his next album."

Akon says he enjoys performing but he prefers behind-the-scenes work. "You're a lot more powerful behind the scenes," he told *Remix.* "It allows you to continue to be creative. When you're out in the open, you got too many people suggesting what you should be doing. When you're behind the scenes, you can always do what you want to do."

Vibe music editor Jon Caramanica applauds Akon's many collaborations, calling his efforts "vertical integration." It's a modern-day way of branching out within the music industry to give yourself a better chance at a long and profitable career.

"Maybe not in a conventional pop-star way, but he'll probably never want for work," Caramanica told China's business newspaper *The Standard.*

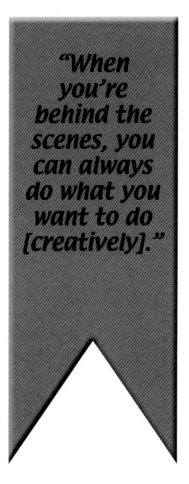

"When you're behind the scenes, you can always do what you want to do [creatively]."

Building His Brand

*A*fter just three years, Akon had sold more than 5.2 million albums worldwide, and his career was showing no signs of cooling off.

"There aren't many mass-appeal male pop stars," Peter Baron, vice president of label relations, music, and talent for MTV Networks told *The Standard* in early 2007. "Justin [Timberlake] is one of them, and Akon is another. It's Akon's moment right now. There's just something about him. He has a different sound, a different look, a different vibe. He's doing something nobody else is doing, blending pop melodies with hip-hop beats and adding Caribbean and African influences. It doesn't hurt that he's great-looking, very stylish, and very likable. It's a magical combination."

Akon's career is not without controversy. For starters, his lyrics are hardly the stuff of Disney movies. His onstage antics, too, have come under fire. Akon made headlines around the world when, at an April 2007 concert, he

Akon attends a radio station-sponsored party in New York City in early 2005. His controversial lyrics and onstage antics have not put a dent in his record sales or radio play.

danced provocatively with the fifteen-year-old daughter of a prominent Trinidad pastor. When video of the onstage dance found its way online, Verizon Wireless pulled its support of the Gwen Stefani/Akon Sweet Escape tour and removed Akon ringtones from its stores and headsets. The communications company also stopped airing V CAST TV spots airing the R&B artist. Additionally, Trinidad's prime minister initiated a formal investigation into the incident. He ultimately ruled Akon's actions were neither lewd nor illegal.

Scandal and dropped sponsors aside, Akon's career has continued to flourish and, like many of today's hottest stars, he's become more than just a musician—he's a brand.

> *"Diamonds are always going to be selling, people are always going to get married, black people will always want to shine and bling, bling."*

While he refuses to glorify his criminal past, Akon says he learned much of what he knows about business from his car-stealing days. Hustlers, he says, have to know what's going to happen before it happens.

These days, Akon is doing his best to stay a couple of moves ahead of the pack. In 2002, the songster teamed up with his friend and manager Melvin Brown to start Konvict Muzik, a label imprint with distribution through Interscope. The label quickly acquired several artists, including Chilli from TLC, Grady Baby, Dolla, and Earl Ray. He also plans to write film scores.

Akon is developing a movie based on his life. He says *ER* actor Mekhi Phifer will play the lead in the film, tentatively titled *Illegal Alien.*

He's got two clothing lines: Konvict Clothing, featuring streetwear, and the more upscale Aliaune. He told London's *The Independent* that his investment in a diamond mine was especially sound because, he said, "Diamonds are always going to be selling, people are always going to get married, black people will always want to shine and bling, bling."

His troubled past behind him, Akon has established himself as one of the music industry's biggest stars. He plans to continue recording and collaborating with other artists, while stretching himself with forays into TV and movies.

He's reportedly turned down offers to do his own reality show version of *Big Love*. And he says he's in negotiations with Viacom for a reality TV show that would see him going from prison to prison to find the next big convict-turned-music star. "It's almost like the flip side of *American Idol,*" he told the *Calgary Sun*. "You find the troubled kids."

"I'm so busy, my head hurts just thinking about it," he told *The Standard*. "But it's really a blessing to have everything happening."

CHRONOLOGY

19??* Akon has never revealed his birth date. Around the time of his birth, his family lives in Missouri.

19??* At age five, Akon and his family move to Florida.

19??* He begins kindergarten at age seven.

19??* The family moves to New Jersey around 1988.

19??* His parents move to Atlanta, Georgia, leaving Akon and his older brother to fend for themselves in New Jersey.

19??* Akon spends time in juvenile detention before graduating from high school.

19??* He moved to Georgia to attend college but drops out after one year.

1993 Akon meets R&B artist Wyclef Jean.

1999 Akon faces federal charges as the ringleader of a national car-theft operation; he is convicted and sentenced to three years in prison.

2002 Akon is released from prison and begins work on what will become his first album. He establishes Konvict Muzik Group with Melvin Brown.

2003 Akon signs with SRC (Street Records Corporation).

2004 Akon releases his debut CD, *Trouble*.

2005 He becomes Senegal's Youth Ambassador.

2006 He releases *Konvicted*.

2007 He teams up with Gwen Stefani for single "Sweet Escape" and goes on tour with her. Akon receives his first Grammy nomination for Best Rap/Sung Collaboration for "Smack That"; Trinidad prime minister investigates Akon's allegedly lewd onstage behavior.

*Akon has kept his age a secret. While the order of his life events are known, exact dates are not.

DISCOGRAPHY

Albums

2006   *Konvicted*

2004   *Trouble*

Sound Track Contributions/Compilations

2005   *Akon: Trio*

Hit Singles

"Smack That" featuring Eminem

"I Wanna Love You" featuring Snoop Dog

"Ghetto"

"Locked Up"

"Soul Survivor" by Young Jeezy, featuring Akon

"Don't Matter"

"Gangsta Bop"

Books

While there are no other books about Akon written for young readers, you might enjoy the following Blue Banner Biographies of other urban artists:

Bankston, John. *Eminem.* Hockessin, Delaware: Mitchell Lane Publishers, 2004.

Boone, Mary. *50 Cent.* Hockessin, Delaware: Mitchell Lane Publishers, 2007.

Torres, Jennifer. *Mary J. Blige.* Hockessin, Delaware: Mitchell Lane Publishers, 2008.

Torres, Jennifer. *Usher.* Hockessin, Delaware: Mitchell Lane Publishers, 2006.

Tracy, Kathleen. *Chris Brown.* Hockessin, Delaware: Mitchell Lane Publishers, 2008.

Works Consulted

"Akon Continues to Outsell the Competition," *Business Wire,* January 19, 2007.

"Akon on Your Radio," Dose.ca, March 5, 2007.

Banda, Tim Kamuzu, "American or Senegalese, Akon's Music Cuts Across All Borders." AllAfrica.com, March 23, 2007.

Brown, Coryn, "Akon: A Whole New Trouble." Vibe.com, October 10, 2006.

Checkoway, Laura, "Akon: Fight to the Top." Vibe.com, March 19, 2007.

Checkoway, Laura. "Akon: The Last Hit Maker." *Vibe,* April 2007, pp. 92–95.

Du Lac, J. Freedom. "Lord of the Ringtone—and More." *The Washington Post,* March 13, 2007.

Godfrey, Sarah. "Life on the Corner: Fresh Hip-Hop with Akon." *The Washington Post,* December 12, 2005, pp C7.

Jones, Steve, "Akon, not 'Trouble,' Is His Middle Name." USA Today.com, October 4, 2004.

Jones, Steve, "R&B's Akon Knows the Score: 2 Hits at Once." USA Today.com, November 3, 2006.

Katz, Laura, "Akon Wants to Break World Record for Biggest Bling." NetMusicCountdown.com, April 10, 2007.

Rosen, Jody, "Lord of the Ringtones." Slate.com, April 10, 2007.

Sanneh, Kelefa. "Breakthrough Hit in a Jailhouse Lament by One Who Knows." *The New York Times,* July 14, 2004, pp. E1.

Sinclair, Tom. "Rap with Conviction." EW.com, August 13, 2004.

Stevenson, Jane. "Akon Has Konviction." CalgarySun.com, March 1, 2007.

Watson, Margeaux. "5 Things You Should Know about Akon." EW.com, January 25, 2007.

Wilson, Tamara. "Freedom Song." Remixmag.com, December 1, 2006.

On the Internet

Akon
http://www.akononline.com

Music Videos, Reality TV Shows, Celebrity News, Top Stories/MTV
http://www.mtv.com/music/artist/akon/artist.jhtml

Akon-AOL Music
http://music.aol.com/artist/akon/535592/main

Senegal, The Land of the Legendary Teranga and Beautiful Touristic Sites
http://www.senegal-tourism.com/

INDEX